I0765024

Persuasive Presentations:

A Pocket Guide to Persuasive Presentations & Public speaking beyond Presentation Design. Public Speaking Playbook for the Exceptional Presenter.

Includes 300+ PPT Templates

Get Marc Roche's Starter Library
FOR FREE

Sign up for the no-spam newsletter and get an introductory book and lots more exclusive content, all for free.

Details can be found at the end of the book.

Copyright © 2019 **Marc Roche**

Copyright © 2018 by Marc Roche. All Rights Reserved.

No part of this persuasive presentations guide may be reproduced, distributed, or transmitted in any form or by any means, including photocopying, recording, or other electronic or mechanical methods, or by any information storage and retrieval system without the prior written permission of the publisher, except in the case of very brief quotations embodied in critical reviews and certain other noncommercial uses permitted by copyright law.

Topics Covered in this guide:

How to give persuasive presentations, public speaking, presentation skills, presentation design and how to be an exceptional presenter.

Roche Publishing Business English Books. All rights reserved

Contents

"Wise men speak because they have something to say; Fools because they have to say something."

Plato.

Contributors & Influencers

I could not possibly list all the people who have influenced me through their work, but I will try to mention a few of the ones who spring to mind in no particular order. These are my business heroes, and without their contribution through their work, I would never have been able to write this book.

If you have never read their books, and are interested in business and entrepreneurship, I implore you to go out, and buy them and read them over, and over again.

Gary Vaynerchuk

Pat Flynn

Dan Meredith

Timothy Ferriss

Dale Carnegie

Danny Rubin

Hassan Osman

Megan Sharma

William Strunk Jr.

Introduction

Confident Communication

Confidence can sometimes desert you when you really need it, but there isn't a single successful professional out there who doesn't have a few cringe-worthy stories about situations where confidence was non-existent and awkwardness took over. We're going to get right down to the core of what makes people confident in their communication and see how you can use the latest research to succeed. However, I want to stress that if you're anything like me, your lack of super-human confidence comes from a tendency to sit on the fence and not fully commit to the things you're doing. If this is true to any extent for you and you feel like it's holding you back, then it's time to change. You're either ALL out, or you're ALL in and you go 1000% into whatever it is that you're doing or saying.

Communicating with confidence is a skill, which means that anyone can develop it. It just takes patience, thicker skin and a willingness to learn from mistakes. It comes down to practice, practice and more practice. No magic, no Ouija boards, and no praying to the sky. Just practice and willingness to not judge yourself, so that you can adapt and learn, the way mother nature intended you to. So get rid of all that bullshit that society has put on you, and go back to basics. Practice, make mistakes, adapt and learn, no judging.

Confidence, emotional intelligence (EQ) and empathy are all closely linked. Emotional intelligence is a trait, which hiring managers, business partners and colleagues value highly, and many successful individuals have it in abundance.

The more emotional intelligence you develop the more able you'll be to prevent those confidence-sucking awkward situations from occurring. Picking-up on what people think is also a vital skill to have for self-reflection and self-guidance. This doesn't mean that you should worry about what people think, but the better you are at picking-up on people's reactions to you, the better you can become at evaluating yourself from a neutral place.

People's reactions to you are valuable feedback that can help you correct mistakes before they cause any damage. Again, this is not to say that you should worry about what people think. There will always be people who like you and people who don't. Crowd pleasers are genuinely liked by few, and genuinely respected by even fewer.

Are Introverts Less Emotionally Intelligent?

There is some debate about what emotional intelligence should or should not include, but that's beyond the scope of this book, as I don't think it's very helpful to sit around debating the semantics. For the purpose of this book, we will define emotional intelligence as your ability to perceive, assess and manage your and other people's feelings appropriately in relation to yourself and the world around you in that moment.

Having a high degree of emotional intelligence will help you have more self-control in emotionally intense situations, and it will help you respond appropriately to your own and other feelings.

It's fair to say that most people are not true introverts or total extroverts, and that instead, they act differently according to how familiar they are with particular situations.

Whether you'd class yourself as a true introvert or just someone who feels less confident when you find yourself in unfamiliar or uncomfortable social settings, the chances are you have a high level of ability when it comes to gauging what people are thinking or feeling. Ironically, it's probably this fine-tuned, bad-ass Bruce Lee, APEX predator-like survival instinct that's holding you back. Let me elaborate…

If you walk around full of self-confidence yet completely oblivious to what other people are thinking or feeling, it may give you the ability to talk to anyone and even to get along with most people on a superficial level. However, you lack an integral APEX predator survival skill, which is being able to read people and gauge social dangers. Without this instinct you're essentially at the bottom of the food chain so to speak.

If you have a highly effective instinct to warn you about potential dangers, your brain is doing its job, and you just need to interpret the message the way it was meant. It's a warning of a potential danger, almost like when you're driving a car and you see a curve ahead.

If we scratch a little deeper under the surface, introverts can have a highly fine-tuned sense of what people are thinking and feeling, which can lead them to being more sensitive and 'shying away' from social situations in business and/or in everyday life.

Contrary to what people often believe, introverts often pick-up on communication signals much better than extroverts, and are better listeners and often rated more highly on their communication skills when they choose to interact.

Leave your ego and worries behind. Being defensive or timid because of pride or fear are two sure-fire ways to FAIL at interacting with people. The simple answer is that it's about practice, practice and more practice. To improve the quality of your interactions you essentially just go out there and interact with people! You will make mistakes and you will learn from those mistakes. This will allow you to adjust and fine-tune your skills.

Emotional Intelligence at Work

Successful people know a great deal about their field of expertise and their job, and the roles of those around them, but it has become clear that to truly succeed, you need more than just the standard intellect.

Emotional intelligence is central to helping you reach your goals and to achieving success, as it boosts your levels of morale, motivation and co-operation (Strickland, 2000).

E.I. is not only being able to identify and adapt to your own emotional state, but the emotions of those around you. An emotionally intelligent individual is a strong communicator who can "read the room" and thrive in a variety of social situations. Many astute hiring managers actively look for this quality when recruiting new staff. There are many reasons, but one of them is that emotionally intelligent employees are generally more successful in their interactions with other members of staff, and as a result, they quickly adapt to many different types of social environments. A good atmosphere in the office is essential and if managed properly, it will lead to increased productivity and employee retention (Lopes, Salovey, & Straus, 2003).

Multiple studies have shown that emotionally intelligent people achieve more than their counterparts both inside and outside of work. They're more likely to handle criticism well and are able to respond appropriately to differences of opinion. In teams, the more emotionally intelligent members help diffuse and prevent emotional outbursts that could derail or delay projects.

A 2014 study conducted by the University of Bonn in Germany set out to find how high emotional intelligence affected an individual. The study was conducted on 142 adults who were asked to identify emotions both through visual and audio cues. Participants were presented with photographs of people and audio of a variety of people expressing their emotions. A 'high emotional intelligence' was defined as being able to correctly identify 87% of the emotional scenarios, a 'low intelligence' was defined as scoring 60% or less.

The participants were then evaluated by their co-workers and supervisors to see how their communication skills were viewed by their peers. The results showed that those with high scores in the test were seen as carrying a higher social status than those who scored lower. Interestingly, those same people who scored higher in the test, also had higher income. Therefore, the study concluded that emotionally perceptive people were viewed more favorably by others and were also more likely to have a higher income than their co-workers.

Regardless of what business you're in, communication with colleagues and clients plays a huge role and that is why emotional intelligence is so valuable. Although the value of emotional intelligence is abundantly clear today, that was not always the case. Travis Bradberry, one of the authors responsible for Emotional Intelligence 2.0 says that emotional intelligence was never considered a factor in business until 1995. His book goes over decades of research to show just what an impact emotional know-how has on the business world.

Don't worry – emotional intelligence is a learned skill and can be improved. The basis of this form of intellect relies on synthesizing information from both the rational and emotional areas of your brain. Like anything else in life, the more you practice emotional intelligence, the stronger that skill will become.

"The change is gradual, as your brain cells develop new connections to speed the efficiency of new skills acquired. Using strategies to increase your emotional intelligence allows the billions of microscopic neurons lining the road between the rational and emotional centers of your brain to branch off small "arms" to reach out to other cells," explains Bradberry.

Each cell in your brain can develop 15,000 connections, which means even the best have lots of room to improve. As you continue to refine your emotional intelligence, you'll find that it gets easier and even automatic at times. When acting with emotional intelligence becomes second nature, you just might find that success comes to you a little more naturally as well.

Chapter 1. Stop Complaining: It's All Your Fault!

Our Genes Contribute to, but Do Not Define, Who We Are.

We're all spectacularly flawed humans, and we all need to be more proactive in some parts of our lives. This chapter comes from my observations, research and personal experience as a teacher, coach and human. I spend a lot of time one on one with many different people on a daily basis, and this gives me a little bit of an insight into our learning process and how we view that process. I've also learnt a few things from other people along the way.

Ideas about biologically defined limits can be life-changing. The idea that you are born a certain way, with a certain set of strengths and weaknesses, can have a profound effect on your motivation and on how you feel about yourself. How your brain actually works is that it adapts and changes to be the best it can be in the environment you're normally in. For instance, if you need to navigate routes on a daily basis, your brain will change its shape and the size of some of its areas to become more efficient at navigating.

Case Study: The Truth about your Public Speaking Skills

A 2007 study of teenage students found that students who thought of intelligence as non-fixed and changeable were more likely to gradually increase their grades for the following two years. Interestingly, students who thought of intelligence as a fixed, 'you are what your born with' factor, saw very little change in their grades (Blackwell et al., 2007).

After the initial tests, the researchers then performed an intervention with some of the low-achieving students. They taught the students about how their brain worked and how learning changes the human brain by creating new connections. They drilled into them that THEY were in charge of controlling this process and that they had the power to change their brain through their daily activities. Amazingly, grades for the group of students who learnt about how their brain worked immediately started to improve, while the grades of the students who hadn't received the intervention carried on getting worse!

This highlights just how important it is for you to fully understand that YOU are in control of how intelligent and talented you are. Your brain is hard-wired to respond to your actions and your environment, so once again YOU are in control.

If you really want to improve your business communications skills and your EQ, it's time to take responsibility for your own learning and your own growth. It's nobody else's responsibility, not your parents', not your partner's, not your boss', not your coach's: it´s you and only you who can succeed. This is your legacy, your blood, your sweat and your tears, no one else´s. I have said this to several students and some have reacted positively and some have given up. I think both decisions were right because it pushed them towards what they really wanted to do deep down.

Nobody can make you learn or do anything, you have to like it and want it. You don't necessarily have to like the thing you are doing in that moment, but you have to love the journey that it forms a part of. I personally don't like learning about marketing analytics, but I know it's useful and I love the process of building businesses, writing and coaching. So in a strange way, when I learn about analytics, I enjoy it because it forms part of my journey and it's almost like scratching an itch.

Decisions = Behaviour

Behaviour is a manifestation of decisions, not conditions. As Franklin Covey stressed in his bestselling book The 7 Habits of Highly Effective People, "Response-ability" is your ability to choose your response to a situation or an environment.

Too many people do the exact opposite and blame their behaviour on their situation or their conditions. Even worse, they blame their current situation on their past situation. This makes them feel like it's not their fault, but is the equivalent of going into a McDonalds today because you went yesterday, and then complaining that you want pizza. Get a grip. If you look at where you are in life now, it's all a product of your decisions and your choices, your job, your level of income, your relationships, your preparation for exams, 100% your fault, the good and the bad.

People who succeed at an activity do not blame their situation for their lack of success, and they definitely don't blame it on a lack of ability. They try, fail and try again in a slightly different way until they succeed.

People who succeed take action and actively learn how they can change things that they wish to change. If they want to learn a language they research how best to learn a language and then they go out there and do it EVERY DAY because they love the process of getting better and challenging themselves. If they want to set up a business they research and research and research and try and fail until they succeed. If you don't already do this, it's definitely not too late, start now.

It comes back to loving the process. If you love what you are doing, then failures and mistakes are not failures or mistakes, they are another step forward in the journey to your inevitable success.

Mistakes and failures are fun, because they are learning opportunities and they teach you more than your successes. If you enjoy what you are doing, then your current situation doesn´t concern you as much, because you are too busy enjoying it.

Understanding the key role of emotion in business separates the best communicators from the rest - not just in terms of results and talents but also in terms of intangible personal assets such as morale, inspiration and dedication. When explaining how great communicators are effective, we describe their strategies, visions, motivation or ideas. However, the reality is that emotions are the crux of great business communication. Leaders understand how to influence emotions and master the art of manipulating them either for good or for evil. It all comes down to how you deal with yourself and your relationships.

Chapter 2. Your Story is Your Vision

What we're about to look at is no secret and is basically common sense, but many people neglect it, or don't fully believe in it enough to implement it. It's based on more than half a century's worth of research into "positive psychology" from institutions including Harvard, Yale and many more.

Imagine for a second we are watching two parallel situations involving two young boys called Jack and Dave. Jack and Dave attend Fleetwood Elementary school in New York, but they don't know each other since it's quite a large school. Jack is feeling anxious and slightly insecure lately. Jack's parents are good parents, but his dad sometimes mocks his intelligence when he makes mistakes. His dad means well, but it makes his son feel stupid at times. Meanwhile, Dave is feeling happy and secure. Dave's parents are supportive and try to reinforce his social confidence at any chance they get.

Today is Wednesday and the school canteen is bustling with voices and laughter, as the dinner ladies serve out the kids' food. Jack sits down with his usual group of friends and starts to eat. He is feeling anxious but can't really pinpoint his feelings as he hasn't experienced them before. He realises he forgot to get a knife and fork for his food, so he stands up to leave the table and as he walks away he hears laughter. He suddenly feels more anxious and embarrassed. 'They noticed I forgot my knife and fork and are laughing because I'm stupid' he thinks. Suddenly, a boy bumps into him. 'He did that on purpose', he thinks to himself. The other boy smiles slyly and apologises. 'He must have heard my friends laughing at me'. Jack feels threatened, so he steps back and scowls, then carries on walking.

All the while, Dave has been sitting with his usual friends in his usual spot and realises he forgot a spoon for his chocolate cake. He stands up and walks away. The table where he was sitting erupts in hysterical laughter. He stops and looks back, he thinks to himself 'I missed a really funny joke, I can't wait to get back to find out what it was'. He runs to get his spoon and bumps into Jack by accident. He apologises. He gets his spoon and returns to the table.

These are cycles, and before the children know it, they have formed deep-set unconscious beliefs about how to interpret other people's actions. If Jack continued in this way without breaking the cycle, he may grow up feeling constantly threatened and guarded.

Should adult-Jack blame his dad for the issues he has? Absolutely not. His dad didn't even do it on purpose, and even if he had, it is adult-Jack who is responsible for his reactions and how he processes his feelings. Jack's cycle could have started for a number of different reasons. The important thing to focus on isn't what random combination of events started Jack's thinking habits and feelings about the people around him, but the fact that they are not real. They are a completely biased and unreliable interpretation of events based on past-experiences and past feelings which were conditioned to happen. If every time I walked down the street I looked at my phone and walked without watching where I was going, when I smashed my face against the nearest lamp-post I wouldn't accept it as a natural part of walking down the street. Smashing my face into a lamp-post was conditioned to happen because of my behaviour and actions. It would happen again and again until I changed my behaviour. The same thing holds true in the case of public speaking. If you don't prepare properly for meetings and presentations, or if you psych yourself out before you speak in public, your negative experience will lead to negative feelings, which in turn will taint your next experience after that and set you up to perform below your potential again.

Thought Patterns & Emotional Intelligence

One of the things emotionally intelligent people do automatically is that they think about whether or not they might be guilty of 'transference'. 'Transference' is when we transfer behaviour and intentions onto other people based on our previous social experiences. When we are more aware of how others may perceive us, and our intentions, or how we ourselves may misunderstand people, we are better equipped to differentiate between "friend or foe". When we are better able to differentiate between real threats and perceived threats, we are free to capitalize on opportunities that present themselves, as we are less preoccupied with our own negative feelings.

We react to everything people say to us in four basic ways, either *positively, neutrally, defensively* or *angrily*. Sometimes our responses are appropriate and sometimes they are a result of incorrectly judging the context of the message we are receiving.

Positive, 'emotionally intelligent' people do something automatically that many people don't even know is possible. They often view the world as having more than one reality or 'story' that is being told, or that could be told. In other words, different versions of the truth in any given situation. They have the ability to detach themselves from the situation and look at it objectively and in a way that is useful for them.

Tell your Story

Our brains are naturally hard-wired to criticize every possible move and critically evaluate every situation. It's arguably a survival mechanism there to protect us from life in the wild. The problem is, we don't need it in such an obvious way anymore, so we misunderstand it. The majority of humans don't go out to hunt in packs anymore. We don't chase down giant beasts and kill them with hand-made weapons and we don't have to fend off wild animals on a daily basis. Our brains are an amazing thing, so they have adapted to our new lifestyles. In that adaptation, they have become critical of our every move so as to produce tactical advantages in today's world. The problem comes when we misinterpret that critical view and we become preoccupied with our own feelings. If your brain is telling you that you didn't do something well, it's not intended to knock you down, it's intended as a warning so that you can perfect your technique and gain a tactical advantage.

The great news is that you can train your brain to see things as they are, no better no worse. Once they are able to do this, they see the situation in their favour and think tactically. This doesn't come naturally to anyone. It comes as a habit that is either instilled in us through our environment and positive thinking cycle (remember Dave) or through practice and hard work. It's one of the most important things you will ever learn to do.

Please note: this doesn't mean you don't see negative situations as they are. It means you realise that depending on how you see these situations, they can help you or damage you. It means that you always find a way to use these 'negative situations' to strengthen you rather than set you back. Whether the glass is half-full or half empty doesn't matter when you trust that you are resourceful enough to find more water.

It's important to understand that every human has insecurities. This is never your fault. However, what you do with the knowledge you have is 100% your choice and your responsibility.

For example:

Reality 1 - Achieving a high score in an aptitude test means you're more intelligent than most people.

Reality 2 - Achieving a high score in an aptitude test means you're more skilled than most people at doing this particular type of test and it only accounts for 25% of job success or income. You have a lot of work to do.

You could argue that both realities are true.

Which type of story sounds more like the ones you tell yourself?

Reality 2 is arguably the most impartial and helpful to anyone who wants to succeed in life.

People with self-awareness and high emotional intelligence often tell the story that benefits them most. If this sounds biased it's because it is, but think about it, if you have to choose between several interpretations of reality, all of which are true, why would you even consider not choosing the most advantageous to you? Why would you ever go out of your way to sabotage yourself and mess your own head up?

How to Identify and Cut Bad Habits

There are two types of things in life: those you cannot influence and those you can influence now. We all worry about a bunch of things every day. As you read this, you might be worried about health, children, problems at work, world peace, or the state of the economy for example.

Many people focus their efforts on the things they are concerned about, which they have no control over yet, which results in accusing attitudes, blaming others, and creating feelings of victimization. They neglect the things they do have control over, so they don´t go forward, and in turn, they feel even worse.

You need to focus all your efforts on the things you have control over now. This is how you grow your knowledge, your confidence and your humanity. Don´t complain, DO.

Be a master of your own improvement. Don´t be a victim of your own bad habits. If you talk to yourself and to others like you are a victim of circumstance, you will never change the things you don´t like or learn the things you want to learn.

So, what do we do with all the failures we've experience in our life? We change those negative memories into positive ones. Using a memory therapy technique that's used to treat PTSD sufferers you can not only remove negative associations from bad memories but actually enhance the positive associations of your good memories.

The method is simple. Take a bad memory, picture it in your mind and slowly allow it to become smaller and dimmer, like the fadeout at the end of a film. Use this dimness to insert new details and rewrite the memory to have a positive spin. You can take a poor presentation you gave and imagine the audience in their underwear, or as a group of monkeys or anything else that might make you smile or make you feel calmer. Keep repeating the memory in your head with these new details and you'll have effectively removed the negative associations.

Apply the opposite method for strengthening positive memories. Bring them to mind and make them bright, loud, and massive in your mind's eye. Keep going over the positive sensations again and again until you feel absolutely unstoppable and let that feeling motivate you.

Do You Talk to Yourself?

Be a master of your own learning. Don´t be a victim of your own bad habits. If you talk to yourself and to others similar to you are a victim of circumstance, you will never change the things you don´t like or learn the things you want to learn.

These are all victim phrases, which should never come out of your mouth or even go through your mind.

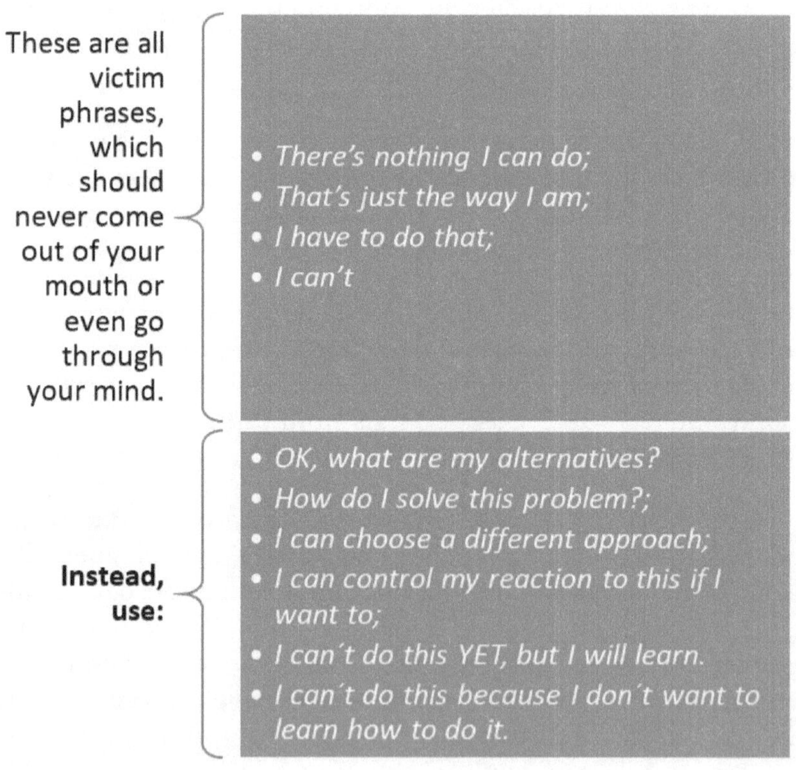

Instead, use:

Whether the glass is half-full or half empty doesn't matter when you trust that you are resourceful enough to find more water.

It's all about the unconscious patterns in your mind. Confident people with high EQ and high self-awareness focus on the story that benefits them most in order to achieve their goals, while people with low self-awareness tend to focus on the story that creates the most pain or anxiety for them.

This is not to say that you should tell yourself that you're going to be a world-champion bull-shark riding ninja, but refuse to practice your ninja skills or your ability to ride bull-sharks. That would be plain delusional. The idea is to be as impartial as possible in your narrative. For example, instead of saying "I can't do this", you could say "I can't do this yet" or "I can't do this because I haven't practiced enough, but I really like it, and I want to practice, so I will", or "I can't do this because I don't like doing it and I don't want to practice!". Be honest and impartial with yourself, it's only fair.

Chapter 3. Voice & the Importance of Sound

"We often refuse to accept an idea merely because the tone of voice in which it has been expressed is unsympathetic to us." –

Friedrich Nietzsche

The Importance of your Voice

Your voice is key when it comes to communicating effectively in business and in non-business settings alike.

Sound can influence the human brain in different ways and it's a vital part of how we understand the world around us and how we interpret different contexts, whether we're aware of it at the time or not.

Projecting your voice appropriately to fit the situation you find yourself in is central to how people perceive your message. Voice control and projection are key, not only for delivering strong presentations, but for exuding confidence in your everyday life. There are a few basic methods you can apply to achieve this, as well as some vocal exercises you can use.

The Psychological Impact of Voice on your Audience

The easiest way to make sure people are listening to you is to talk in a manner that makes them want to listen. Your tone of voice plays a key role in having people not only listen to what you're saying, but to understand it as well. Tone is comprised of a few key elements: pitch, volume, pace, and emphasis.

People have an instinctive reaction to the tone of someone's voice and you want that reaction to be positive. Think of someone you've heard that has an inviting quality to their voice. A popular example is actor Morgan Freeman. He has a rich, deep, expressive voice that naturally draws attention. His voice alone has given him access to an immense amount of opportunities, including the narration of several documentaries. Contrast that with the voice of someone you don't like to listen to: they're often monotone, nasally, and unappealing overall. Even if what they're saying to you has value, you're less likely to accept their message based on the tone of their voice. We've all had teachers whose voices we just couldn't stand. The right tone of voice can be all it takes to propel you forward.

So, when thinking about your own tone try to emulate the voices of those who successfully capture your attention. This does not mean you should be doing an impression of someone else, but simply working within the natural range of your own voice. You should not have to strain yourself or your vocal cords to achieve a desirable tone.

People who speak in a deeper voice are considered to have more authority than others according to research done by the University of Pittsburgh. Some theorize this connection comes from when physical power was used as a measure of authority and a deep voice generally went hand in hand with a stronger body. So, when you're looking to command the attention of others it's important to use the lower range of your voice, without going so far as to put on a cartoonish voice.

Speaking deeply doesn't mean speaking flatly though. It's important to change your tone as you speak to maintain interest and convey emotional information. Without a variance in tone, it becomes nearly impossible to communicate your excitement, enthusiasm, or even successfully land a joke. If your tone is as flat as a piece of paper then it won't matter how deep your voice is, it's going to put people to sleep.

Perhaps the easiest technique for holding people's attention is to simply speak slower and to emphasize the most important words in each sentence. Not only does it give you more time to think through what you're saying, it gives the listener more time to let your message sink in and truly understand it. It takes effort to actually listen to what someone is saying, so giving your listener more time will help the both of you immensely. Don't be afraid to take a long pause between thoughts as well. A silent moment commands authority much better than attempting to fill the silence with "um" or "uh."

When prepping for your next big presentation, meeting or conversation just remember to talk low, slow, with emphasis and with varied tone.

Vocal Warmups

Right off the bat, it's important to breathe through your diaphragm, and stay relaxed around your head, neck and shoulder areas. You may need to make a conscious effort to do this initially, but you'll notice how, as you form the habit, it will become more automatic.

Our first exercises are going to focus on volume. Increasing the volume of your voice to be louder is an essential aspect of projecting your voice. Be sure you're practicing breathing from your diaphragm. Your abdominal area should expand outwards as you breathe in, and contract as you breathe out to get the best results.

We begin using vowel sounds. Starting with "ah" (as in the word "bar") you will begin vocalizing the sounds softly, and gradually increasing your volume to be loud. Make sure you do this somewhere private or you'll lose all your friends.

It's important to understand that when you're loud, you should not be shouting. Think of the difference between talking to someone directly in front of you, and someone a few feet away. That should be the difference between your soft and loud voice.

Reverse the exercise and go from loud to soft.

If you're feeling a strain on the loud end of things, then you're trying too hard. Remember to be gentle.

Finally, combine the exercises and go from soft to loud to soft to loud, etc. for as long as you like.

This exercise can be done with other vowel sounds such as "oo" (as in "boo"), "oh" (as in "hole"), "aw" (as in "raw"), "ay" (as in "bay") and "ee" (as in "see").

Counting to ten is also an effective volume exercise. You can move gradually, starting soft at 1 and ending loud at 10 or vice versa. You can also make a pattern, having every third number spoken loudly or something similar to that. Play around with it and find what works best for you. Have fun and make it part of your routine.

Voice Projection Exercise

Using a combination of single words, phrases, and sequences you will learn how to project by intoning words and phrases. This means you will emphasize and lengthen vowel sounds, which should create a richer sound. When choosing words and phrases be sure to use words that start with the same sound ("my moaning mother's magnificent mistake"). Watch to make sure you don't tense up the muscles in your head and neck as you perform this exercise. Remember to relax.

Of course, vocal projection can be difficult to master and improper practice of these techniques could damage your vocal cords. If you do not feel confident performing these exercises yourself, or if you begin to feel any discomfort or strain, then stop immediately and find yourself a vocal coach to help you with your technique.

Now that we've seen the importance of sound in communication, let's take a look at some of the barriers our interactions face.

Chapter 4. Posture

"Body language and tone of voice - not words - are our most powerful assessment tools." -

Christopher Voss

Be aware of your posture.

Pop stars, charismatic politicians and actors, are often admired based on the idea that they were born with a special talent for performing. Though there may be some natural talent involved, performance is a set of skills and always has been. This means that you can learn.

It's not magic or woo woo energy, it's science. The brain adapts and learns to the environment to which it's subjected. If you practice, you improve.

Certain habits can make you voice tense, which has a negative impact on your performance as a communicator. If you constantly slouch because you're always looking down at your phone or laptop, this will affect your voice, as you'll be placing extra stress on the neck and voice box area. Try to stand up straight as much as possible and try to monitor and correct your posture as much as possible.

Combine breathing through your diaphragm, and staying relaxed around your head, neck and shoulder areas with a good posture – that means no leaning or slouching regardless of whether you're standing or sitting – and you'll be in a prime position to make vocal projection as easy as possible.

To help keep your posture in check, use an action or event that occurs regularly in your life, such as checking your phone, as a reminder to check in on your posture. Check to see that you're relaxed, your spine is straight, and you're not accidentally clenching your teeth or unnecessarily straining parts of your body.

It's important to remember that projecting your voice should not be causing any strain on your cords or any other part of your body. If you feel any strain, then you're not projecting, you're yelling. Remember to focus on being gentle with your vocal cords as you practice and to reassess your technique if you start to feel any strain.

Chapter 5. Barriers to Effective Communication

"The most important thing in communication is hearing what isn't said." –

Peter Drucker

What's in it for them?

The world is full of constant distraction in the form of media, entertainment, social interaction and many, many other things. People automatically grab for their phones whenever they have a spare few seconds. Even billboards are becoming less and less relevant as a marketing tool since most people's attention while they sit in cars is now down towards their phones.

Why should they listen to you? Why should anybody listen to anyone else?. *"What's in it for me?"* - This is what we all instinctively ask ourselves when we start reading something or listening to someone.

It's not just about what you have to say, it's about how you deliver your message and about whether your message is valuable to your audience. You need to be helping your audience in some way for them to stick with you. This is what you should be focused on when you speak, write and present.

In a world where attention is so fickle, if you want people to listen to you, you need to grab them and keep them long enough for them to hear your message. There is constant temptation to become distracted, so you need to get good at the attention game.

If one were to seek out an unconventional definition of communication, it would be, Brain to Brain marketing, since communication is the meeting of minds. Communication is devoid of words, sentences, paragraphs and the entire spectrum of linguistic tools and methods. In its truest form, it is two nervous systems exchanging information. It is effective when the circumstances are as unbounded as possible.

Using Meaningless Language:

We're all guilty of this now and again, but it really is a communication killer because it sucks the power and meaning out of whatever it is you're saying.

Sometimes we resort to hyperboles, like "incredible" and "awesome" to talk about relatively uninteresting things, such as when someone has bought a new hat. We often do this to please others or make them feel at ease, but while it may be intended as a gesture of goodwill towards the other person, it can come off as insincere and can shape other people's perception of what we consider to be "incredible". If everything is "incredible" then nothing we describe will ever truly be incredible.

Ego

Another thought pattern that damages the effectiveness of our communication is our fear of being seen to be wrong. When we're overly concerned by this, it can distort our interpretation of the messages we get from other people and from our environment. This will in turn, influence our response.

People Pleasing and Seeking Approval

People pleasing, or seeking approval from others is another surefire way to damage and distort your communication at work.

Although peer pressure is probably more obvious among teens, it definitely carries on into adulthood in more subtle and unconscious ways. We buy certain things to keep up with the Jones' and we all say certain things to be seen in a certain light to some extent, whether we admit it to ourselves or not. If we let this behavior get out of hand, we become people pleasers and others see straight through this. People pleasers often come across as insincere and manipulative. People will not respect our message if they do not respect our values.

Difficult and emotional situations:

Another potential impediment to effective communication is the way we deal with stressful and emotional situations.

Our instinctive reaction is often to stay silent in order not to make things worse. Remaining silent and not acknowledging the factors involved in a situation can cause more harm than good and can lead to serious misunderstandings of both the events and the emotions surrounding it.

Chapter 6. The Neuroscience of World-Class Presentations

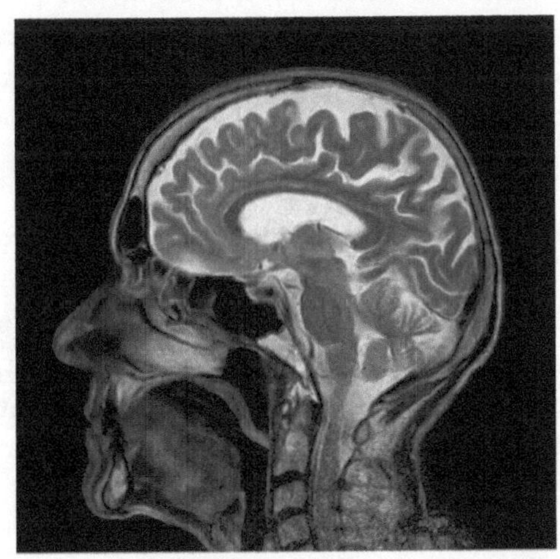

The Multi-Modal Technique

Engaging with material in multiple formats, such as combining text with a visual representation, can improve your audience's memory of the concepts or ideas being presented (Paivio and Csapo, 1973). Hardly rocket science is it, but so many of us throw common sense straight out of the window the minute we sit down to plan a presentation.

This is what the idea of multimodal education is based on. Multimodal education emphasizes combining learning methods in order to better teach students. This technique has been proven to increase brain activity beyond the point of what using a singular method can produce (Beauchamp et al., 2004).

More important than an increase in brain activity is where that activity takes place. Studies saw increased activity in the superior temporal sulcus and middle temporal gyrus, which are both responsible for multisensory processing. The fact that this region of the brain switches on automatically when exposed to multiple stimuli suggests that it plays a large part in the improved memory that results from multisensory exposure.

So say you have a presentation coming up, try to combine images or even short videos (if appropriate), with small amounts of clearly expressed text and speaking. Keep shifting between the different 'modes' to keep your audience's brains as active as possible.

The positive effects of combining mediums on memory can be seen in a study in which participants had their brains scanned as they were given a memory test where they had to memorize pairs of objects. After the test, participants filled out a questionnaire about what memorization techniques they used to help them complete the task. Though self-reporting can be an unreliable method of gathering information, the brain imaging showed that people who combined auditory information with the images they saw, techniques as simple as saying the names of the objects they saw aloud, performed better than those who didn't. The study concluded that engaging with material in multiple different ways made a stronger impact on the people's memories (Kirchhoff and Buckner, 2006).

Using Stress to Enhance Memory

Another factor that can have a positive effect on learning and memory recall is physical and psychological stress. Interestingly, stress must be occurring at the same time as the event that you wish people to recall or learn, for the memory enhancement to happen (Joels et al., 2006). Stress that occurs before or after the event has been shown to actually be detrimental to memory (de Quervain et al., 2000; Kirschbaum, 1996; Kuhlmann, 2005).

This doesn't mean that you should make your presentations ultra-stressful by shouting at people or by setting off the sprinklers on them, but it does mean that you can benefit from adding a small element of stress through practical simulations or activities for instance. During your simulations, you could add something as simple as a time limit to inject low levels of stress and excitement.

The effects of physical stress, including things like hunger, or extreme temperatures, activate the lower regions of the brain which typically govern more basic body processes. Psychological stress, such as that from receiving bad news, targets areas of the brain associated with higher function, such as the amygdala and the limbic regions in general (Herman and Cullinan, 1997).

The brain responds to psychological stress by producing noradrenaline, which mobilizes the brain and body to take action. The key with psychological stress is that it increases memory for what caused the stress, but not for information unrelated to that stress (McGaugh, 2004). This means that the timing and cause of the stress can make a huge difference as to whether its effects on memory will be positive or negative.

'Chunking' Information

When we look at memory, we often undervalue factual recall and muscle memory, but advances in neuroscience have shown that these play a huge factor in maintaining what is called "working memory." Working memory serves as a temporary store for new information we are processing. The average limitation on a working memory is roughly seven individual pieces of information though this number can vary based on the individual and their educational achievements (Pickering, 2006). Our working memory is what we use for everything from writing down a phone number (which is why we often like to get the info in small pieces rather than all at once) to learning a new skill or concept. Try to use this knowledge when you present information so you don't overload and ultimately lose your audience. Deliver the information to your audience in small digestible chunks so that they can process it.

A 2003 study used functional magnetic resonance imaging (fMRI) to track the regions of the brain that adults were using as they learned to do long-form multiplication (Delazer et al., 2003). The study saw brain activity shift from the region associated to working memory to the region associated with automatic function as the adults practiced the skill and familiarized themselves with it. This study shows how the brain relies on different regions depending on its familiarity with the task at hand and it also shows why it's important to keep your working memory in good nick to allow it to grasp new ideas quickly and effectively. It's also worth noting that external representation of information (such as the written down phone number or a written-out math equation) can help take pressure off of the working memory and increase efficiency, as your brain will be able to focus better on the task. This is similar to when you close down unnecessary programs on your computer to free up the CPU and the system. As result of this, the computer speeds up and can process tasks faster.

Educating Through Imitation and Visualization

It's common knowledge in the worlds of sport and psychology that visualization is an incredibly effective tool for learning.

Visualizing an object activates your brain and mirrors the activity of your brain actually seeing the object in real life (Kosslyn, 2005). As far as far as your brain is concerned, you're actually seeing whatever it is that you're visualizing.

The effectiveness of visualization techniques comes from the "mirror neuron system" in our brains, which focuses on learning and mimicking the actions of other humans (van Gog et al., 2008). Research has shown that this kind of observation activates the same regions in the brain that activate when we actually perform the action! (Rizzolatti and Craighero, 2004). This is what enables us to learn by copying when we are young. During our childhood our mirror neuron system is hyper-stimulated, which is why toddlers tend to copy everything they see and hear! The same region is activated even when we have an action explained to us (Tettamanti et al., 2005).

Chapter 7. Listen!

"There is a difference between listening and waiting for your turn to speak."-

Simon Sinek

Emotional Intelligence and Empathy

Psychologist Edward Thorndike spoke of "social intelligence" as the ability to understand people and social relationships. Just as attempts have been made to measure intellectual ability in the form of Intelligence Quotient or IQ tests, so have we attempted to understand emotional intelligence with EQ tests. Empathy is one of the main qualities found in emotionally intelligent people. Empathy is not exactly the same as sympathy although the two are very similar.

Think of empathy as "Advanced Sympathy"

Sympathy means recognizing someone's pain and responding accordingly and consciously with some form of support, for example with hugs or reassurance. But the person feeling sympathetic is still somewhat of an outsider to the actual emotions being experienced and felt. Empathic people literally feel the similar emotions to the people they are around. For example, they don't just feel sorry for someone - they feel that person's sorrow as their own. Parents usually have a somewhat empathic connection to their children.

Research on empathy shows that just as psychopathic behavior has neurobiological roots, there is a part of the brain called the right Supramarginal Gyrus, which recognizes instances where there is no empathy and corrects this behavior. What is interesting is that in instances where quick decisions need to be made, this area of the brain doesn't function as well as it usually does, reducing our ability to empathize. This is an actual observable phenomenon as scientists are able to see which areas of the brain light up more during certain situations through scans. When certain parts of a patient's brain are damaged, we've been able to see the results in the changed behavioral patterns of that person. Some brain lesions can disrupt a patient's ability to interpret body language or to share and understand other people's emotions, creating an inability to empathize. (Hillis, & E., A. 2013).

The Truth about Empathy

"Try first to understand" before you try to be understood. Or in other words, "listen" more than you speak.

We are all guilty of this, we like the sound of our voice at times and we speak more than we listen. True empathetic listening, is listening with the intention of understanding.

Empathy is a great attribute to have, not only because it makes you a better human. Something I learnt through teaching and coaching, is that empathetic listening is powerful, NOT because "it's what nice people do", or because "it's the right thing to do". Those things are true, but empathetic listening is powerful because it provides you with accurate data on the person or group you are interacting with.

In order to truly help another person and make a difference in their life, whether it´s in your professional or in your personal life, you need accurate data. Obviously, getting to know other people and learning about their stories is very interesting in itself. However, the practical value lies in the data they are giving you about themselves. How can you achieve a win/win unless you have the data? The answer is, in my experience, you can't.

The Basic Dynamics of Interaction

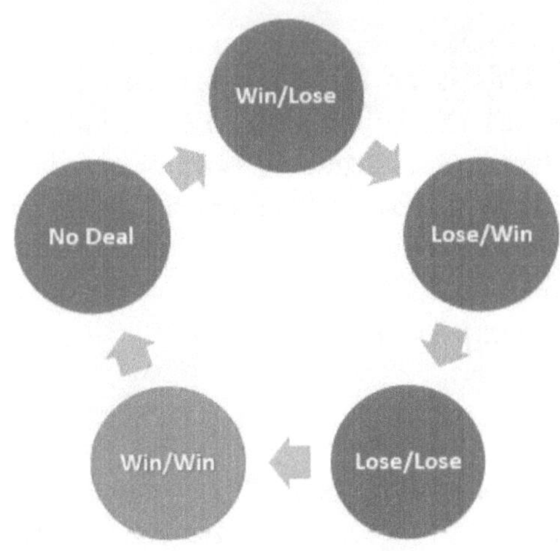

In his bestselling book *The 7 Habits of Highly Effective People: Powerful Lessons in Personal Change*, Stephen R. Covey presents these five possible results of human interaction. They represent the mentality and possible general outcomes of any interaction between human beings. The sixth paradigm "Win", is missing, because a "Win" mentality, when someone doesn´t care about the outcome as long they win, inevitably leads to one of the other paradigms. □

Win/Win. — is a way of thinking, which tries to bring value to other people without accepting injustice. Interactions with other people are not battles but collaborations for mutual benefit and value.

Win/Lose. — This is an attitude that tries to establish a situation where you win and the other side loses. While this is necessary in competition and war, it is arguably only beneficial in these particular situations, and not in everyday interactions (business or personal). For example, win-win with employees, colleagues, partners and customers is far more effective and beneficial long term. Win-lose might be appropriate with competitors for example.

Lose/Win. — This is what gave "nice guys" a bad reputation. The problem is, real nice guys don´t play this game. This game is more for "scared guys". When someone allows people to do things in order to avoid confrontation, it can cause a lot of damage to everyone involved.

Lose/Lose. — This is when two win-lose people, departments or businesses get together. Nobody wins here.

No Deal. — the interaction may lead to no agreement or no production of value to any side. This is a No Deal.

What are Win-Win people like?

They have integrity — they value themselves as a person of consistency and have a specific moral code, which they follow.

They are mature — they have an understanding of the world, from a "big picture" standpoint

They have an abundance mentality — there is plenty out there for everyone. We can all benefit from this opportunity!

Empathetic listening:

Empathetic listening creates stronger relationships and improves information processing in the brain.

1. Put the feelings and thoughts of others before your own

2. Let your guard down and be open with your emotions and opinions

3. Imagine yourself in the experiences and perspectives of others

4. Avoid judgment or criticism while being receptive

If you apply these principles you'll understand people's emotions better and, as a result, build closer more meaningful relationships. The more you apply these principles the more people will want to share with you, try it and see.

Chapter 8. Your Words Matter

"As we express our gratitude, we must never forget that the highest appreciation is not to utter words, but to live by them." -

John F. Kennedy

Think About Your Words

When focusing on improving our presentation skills we often look at some of the best presentations in order to mimic the techniques of icons like Steve Jobs, or VaynerX's Gary Vaynerchuk, but it can be just as valuable to look at bad presentations to see what kind of mistakes we should avoid.

The words you say also matter. Always think that in a professional environment your words can be misconstrued or taken out of context. Be very careful with edgy comments and speeches!

We'll take a look at a couple arguably dreadful speeches and presentations to see what went wrong, and what can be done to avoid these scenarios ourselves. These speeches are listed in Vanessa Ong's excellent 2017 article *15 Bad Speeches We Can Learn From.* I urge you to check it out when you have a minute ☺

Speech Case 1: Miss Teen South Carolina 2007

Take an infamous speech made during the Miss Teen South Carolina show in 2007.

A part of the Miss Teen competition demands that participants answer a "thought-provoking question" in order to demonstrate their higher thinking abilities. The questions are selected at random and Miss South Carolina was asked the following: "Recent polls have shown that one fifth of Americans can't locate the US on a world map, why do you think this is?"

She begins by slowly explaining that some "US Americans" don't have maps and she ends with a vague suggestions that the United States education system should somehow benefit South Africa and Iraq. This is what happens when you charge headlong into a question you are completely unprepared for.

Before we scoff at Miss Teen Carolina, let's get off our high-horse and be honest with ourselves, I'm sure most of us can recall a situation when we've jumped head-first into answering a question and then realized half-way through that we're talking absolute nonsense. It can be a horrible, embarrassing feeling when this happens. So, what can we learn from this?

Lesson 1: Be prepared.

Managing a presentation requires you to be aware of two things: the message you want to deliver to your audience, and the information your audience might want from you. During election campaigns, politicians have to be able to speak on a variety of different issues, from education to environmental policy and more. If you prepare yourself in a similar fashion, then you'll drastically decrease your odds of being caught out during a big moment.

Lesson 2: Take your time when answering a question.

You are under no obligation to answer questions as quickly as possible; it's a presentation, not a race. Do not be afraid to ask someone to repeat their question or to pause and consider the question before answering. If you truly don't have an answer for someone, be honest with them and tell them you will get back to them after you find the answer. Not only will you avoid embarrassment in front of an audience, but you'll come off as thoughtful and honest. People respect honesty and "cojones", so show them you have both!

Speech Case 2: Melania Trump's Republican National Convention Speech

Melania Trump's Republican National Convention Speech

The speech Melania Trump gave at the 2016 Republican National Convention was widely spread around the internet not because it was an incredible speech, but because it was almost a word-for-word copy of a speech previously given by Michelle Obama. Videos went up online directly comparing the two and the evidence is quite damming.

It is a good thing to be inspired by the works of others. It's even smart to bring their work into your own presentation, but you have to do it properly. Always cite your source, give credit where credit is due, and make it abundantly clear when you are using someone else's words to support your point. Remember, people came to hear your words, not to hear you parrot the words of others.

If Melania Trump had talked about how Michelle Obama's speech had affected her own views and simply incorporated quotes into her speech, then it would've likely been received as a groundbreaking political speech and would have been used as a shining example of respect. Melania would have come off as a big person who was brave enough to admit that she was inspired by a political rival and brave enough to show public respect and appreciation for her. This rarely happens in politics, so it would have been big news for all the right reasons.

There are thousands of pitfalls to watch out for in public speaking, but if you use a little common sense and take things slowly then you should be able to perform pretty well on the day.

Chapter 9. Eye Contact

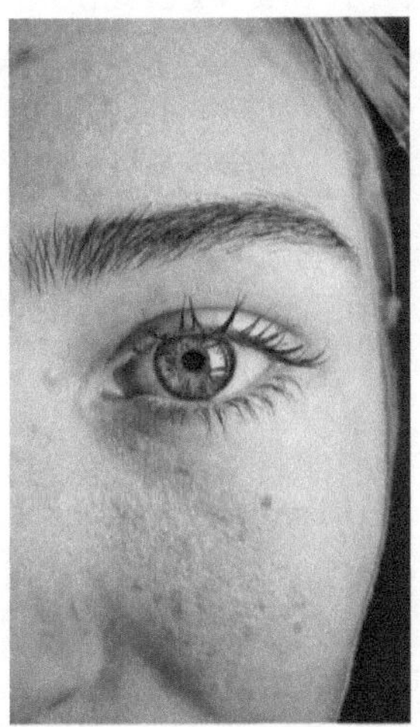

The importance of eye contact in Western cultures is undeniable. Neglect eye contact and your audience will assume you lack confidence at best and that you are untrustworthy at worst.

It's easy to mess up and really hard to do properly. If you do it too much it becomes threatening; but then, not enough of it can have the same effect. This is the exact reason why one-on-one interactions often go hand-in-hand with private brain meltdowns *"Do I make eye contact again now? Is it too much? How long is acceptable before looking away?"*

In a study done by Japanese researchers, volunteers watched a video of someone's face whilst solving a word challenge in which they had to think of verbs to match different nouns. For example if they heard "ball" the word "kick" would be logical.

Amazingly, as soon as the face in the video appeared to be making eye contact with them, the volunteers started having problems with the more difficult nouns. Even with a stranger in a video, eye contact is so powerful that it uses the person's cognitive reserves, leaving him or her unable to effectively concentrate on anything else!

Practice gazing towards your audiences' face or faces to strengthen the connection while you're delivering your message, but don't worry too much about making actual eye contact all the time. A recent study using eye-tracking technology carried out by ECU researchers gave surprising results as to the importance of eye contact.

During the study, one of the researchers engaged short four-minute conversations with 46 test subjects. In the conversations, both people wore eye-tracking goggles. For around 50% of the interactions the person conducting the tests looked at the subject's eyes the majority of the time, and for the other 50% he gazed mostly at the mouth.

Following each of the conversations, the volunteers evaluated how much they enjoyed the interactions. In the conversations where the researcher had been looking mainly at the volunteers' mouths, they reported the same levels of eye contact and enjoyed the interactions just as much as when the researcher made direct eye contact.

This research suggests that gazing at people's face produces the same effects as direct eye contact. So if you're not 100% comfortable with making confident eye contact all the time don't get too hung up on it. There's no need to try to make eye contact with your audience, instead just gaze at their faces.

Chapter 10. Dawn of the 'Corpobots'

We're living in a connection economy where people want to connect with real people. The old business jargon for the sake of business jargon of yesteryear has been demoted to the boardrooms where it's still needed for political games. To connect with humans, you need words that make you sound like a real human, sentences that show who you are, why you're doing what you're doing and why you're different to the 'corpobots'.

When humans switch into the "business" mindset, something dark and strange happens to their brain, they become flesh and bone robots morphing their vocabulary into a meaningless collection of clichés and empty statements - the result is just boring, vague and disjointed communication.

We place greater importance on how someone talks than on the words they are saying alone. Good speaking and writing don't usually do the whole hard-selling approach. They use accessible language as much as possible and focus on adding value, reducing pain or discomfort by solving problems and satisfying a need.

What is your Audience's Pain-Point or Need?

Think about what problems or 'personal hells' your audience is experiencing at the moment. Again, by audience, I mean anybody you interact with for business or professional reasons. It could be a one-to-one negotiation, a sales email or a presentation among many other situations. Think about what personal misery your idea, or product or service saves your audience from. Then, think of all the benefits that they will gain from it and how that will feel. Don't just describe features and benefits of your idea and hope for the best, show them how it feels. Why does your idea matter to them?

<u>GOUSTO UK</u>

This is a perfect example of a company using pain points to show how a product or service solves a 'personal hell'. Think of the 'personal hell' of having to go to do the weekly shop as a single parent of two children with no childcare and no car for example.

Notice how they use the pain-points to empathize with the audience, create rapport and offer the solution. Notice also how they use simple, direct and clear language without any pretense.

This is an excerpt from the "help" section of Gousto's website. https://www.gousto.co.uk/help

'With Gousto you don't need that epic shopping list, soul-crushing queue at the checkout or to take part in the heavyweight grocery bag Olympics. All you need is your weekly box.'

Always Give Details

Giving details is what separates a boring generic text or conversation and a lively, interesting interaction. If possible, try to give extra details and be as specific as you can in your interactions without being anal of course.

For example, say "Pizza Marinara" instead of just "pizza", or say "Northern Pikes" instead of "Fish". You get the idea.

Details are particularly important when you're trying to sell solutions to your audience. It really helps in presentations, testimonials and case studies.

BLU HOMES

This is a great example of a company using details to convey personality and uniqueness. This style lends itself well to presentations, website copy, catalogues and even certain types of emails and meetings.

The following excerpt is from the "Why Blu" section of Blu Home's website. https://www.bluhomes.com/why-blu

The future of home building has arrived.

Unique Innovative Design.

A Blu home is like nothing else. We have been innovatively designing our homes from the ground up for the last 10 years. We design homes to be lived in, with open spaces, lots of windows and floor plans that make sense. You will never look at building a home "the old way" again.

Faster to Build

Our homes are factory built and finished on your site in less than 3 months. Custom homes typically take over 1 year, talk about game changing.

Notice how they give details but keep it simple and clear at the same time. They clearly capitalize on the benefits of Blu Homes over other pre-fab houses on the market.

Chapter 11. Any Fool Can Complicate

"Any fool can make something complicated. It takes a genius to make it simple."

Woody Guthrie

Communicating Clearly

The techniques looked at so far won't do much good unless your message is clear and concise. Language is a powerful force and it can be used to help or to confuse and damage. The problem comes when we wrongly confuse the language used to confuse and damage with good communication.

In this section, you'll learn the principles of clear, powerful business communication. In the process of doing this, you'll not only improve your speaking and writing skills; you'll hopefully see the beauty and importance of clarity.

Can you think of anything more mind-numbingly frustrating than struggling through a business contract, trying to make sense of the unnecessarily dull legal speak while dealing with crucial things you need to know?. Or desperately attempting to remain focused while you're reading a pompous academic paper on what would have been a gripping topic, had the researcher written it thinking about the reader?

Clarity = Confidence

Clarity shows confidence and respect for your audience. People see straight through jargon and unnecessarily complex language in a heartbeat. They often assume that you don't know what you're talking about, that you're nervous, or in the worst case scenario, that you're pretentious, insecure and incompetent. Chances are you're none of the latter, so remember that less is more. Of course, 'clarity' isn't about dumbing it down for your audience, it's about making it easy for them, it's about being your audience's advocate.

In academic and political settings, the tendency is to complicate concepts and make them less accessible. This is often done unconsciously in academia, as this world has developed a standardized style which peers have come to expect from each other. Though it may be tradition to complicate concepts in the hope of making them seem more 'academic' or 'professional', or in order to justify one's own research grant, it's of little use when you want to reach other humans and create meaningful connections.

What do Winston Churchill, Barack Obama and Adolf Hitler have in common?

They all told a good story and they all won people over through simple language and clear messaging. Regardless of politics, all three men were extremely effective communicators who people listened to.

Even if you look at the most respected business magazines and newspapers in the world, you'll find that they prioritise simplicity and directness. The Economist style guide emphasizes that the "first requirement of The Economist is that it should be readily understandable. Clarity of writing usually follows clarity of thought. So think what you want to say, then say it as simply as possible."

Example:

"Improving the efficacy of measurable learning outcomes" could be expressed as "improving learning" or "improving learning efficiency" if you want to complicate it a bit more. There is definitely no need for the empty self-indulgent language used in the original version. Remember that clichés and vagueness are for people who don't know what they're talking about.

Exercise:

Read the following text and change it to make it more personal, direct and interesting. I've provided an example at the end of the exercise so you can check, but there are many ways of rewriting this paragraph. (Please note that this not a real example and any resemblance to any real companies is purely coincidental).

Original text:

"The staff at XYZ Media have been consulting successfully and fostering measureable, tailored solutions for their clients for years. The company's highly experienced media consultants understand and appreciate their clients' requirement to launch and implement cost-effective cutting-edge solutions strategically and systematically. Their sensitivity to the client's objectives, together with their profound expertise in marketing strategy and social media bring added-value and synergy to any project they embark upon."

OK, let's see if we can clean it up a bit…

Write your version here:

....

....

....

....

....

....

....

....

....

....

....

Sample Answer

"We've been helping our clients make profit off advertising and social media for years. Our experienced specialists understand and appreciate your need to increase profits and brand recognition by implementing cost-effective solutions logically and systematically. Our sensitivity to your objectives, together with our expertise in marketing strategy and social media will help you achieve your objectives"

Notes:

This sample is by no means perfect. There is still some work that needs to be done, but it's better than the original.

The first thing we've done here is that we've simplified it. We've cut any words that didn't add to the message. Words like *"synergy"* have been cut altogether.

The second thing we've done here is we've reworded some of the business jargon to make it more relatable. There is still some jargon left in this text, but we've tried to reduce it to a minimum. The reader or listener is human, regardless of whether he/she is the cleaner or the CEO of the company. Remember this.

The third thing we've done is, instead of speaking in third person about the company all the time, we've introduced personal pronouns like "we" and personal possessive pronouns like *"our"* and *"your"*.

Finally, we've tried to be as specific as possible. We've talked about *"profits"* and *"brand recognition"* rather than *"measureable, tailored solutions"*. This not only adds to our overall message, but it also adds credibility and makes us more relatable as a business or business professional.

Clear Communication Checklist:

1. Keep your sentences simple and direct

2. Remove unnecessary business jargon to make your communication more effective and powerful. Remember that no matter who you're writing or speaking to, they are human, so relate to them as a human.

3. Avoid the third person if possible. Speak about "us" and "you" if possible.

4. Be as specific as possible. Don't ramble on about *"measureable, tailored solutions"* when your audience is interested in *"profits"* and *"brand recognition"*

5. Avoid the Passive Voice like the plague, unless you have no choice. Instead of saying *"the project was launched by Gary"* use an active sentence like *"Gary launched the project"*. Active sentences tend to sound more alive and as a result more interesting.

Chapter 12. The Neuroscience of Performance Boosting

The Neuroscience of "Practice Makes Perfect"

Effective Business Communication is made-up of a set of skills you can learn. There is no magic involved and no innate talent. Poor communication skills are simply 'learnt behavior', which you can correct and relearn.

Your brain is flexible like plastic. This means that its structure and connections literally change and adapt as you experience the world around you. This is not some theoretical or mental wooh wooh change, it's actual physical change. Changes in size, shape and structure.

While the biggest changes occur during your childhood and teenage years, it doesn't stop there. For instance, when structural MRI scans of the brains of experienced London taxi drivers were analyzed and compared to the brains of people who didn't drive taxis, researchers found that the posterior hippocampi of the taxi drivers were quite a lot bigger when compared to those of the non-taxi drivers. The posterior hippocampus plays a key role in navigation and mapping. The taxi driver's brains had adapted and actually physically developed to suit their daily routine!

Your brain's continuing plasticity appears to be perfect for lifelong learning, which allows you to adapt to new situations and experiences.

In another study in 2004, a group of adults were studied at the start and at the end of a three-month juggling course. The researchers found that the brain areas associated with the activity had grown considerably by the end of the three-month course. Scientist then asked the participants to rest for three months and scanned their brains after the three-month rest period. Astonishingly, after three months of rest from juggling, the participants' brain regions associated with the juggling had shrunk almost to their original pre-training course size (Draganski et al., 2004).

Use Functional Learning to Boost Performance

Functional learning is essentially practical learning, where you perform tasks to achieve a specified result, rather than just study or memorize information.

1. Functional learning mirrors reality.

In a functional learning exercise, you solve a real problem, typically one that mirrors a challenge you face in real life or work, by using the skills you have to apply every day. This bridges the gap between theory and practice.

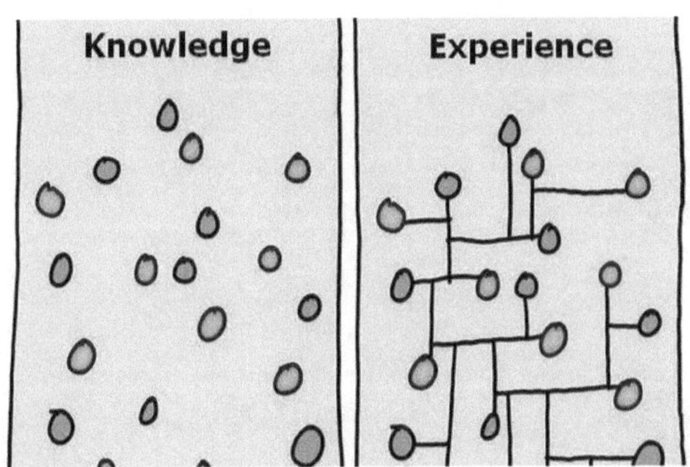

2. Functional learning produces predictable learning.

Functional learning does not happen by accident. A desired goal may include learning new principles, like the importance of planning, or new practices, like how to be a better presenter. Regardless of the objective, the functional learning exercise revolves around instilling those principles or practices in ourselves.

You never just "wait and see what happens." The learning objectives are designed in advance and incorporated into the process to ensure relevance in the real world. Functional learning exercises are carefully calibrated to produce certain results based on the behaviors and decisions that a you make. Thanks to predictable learning outcomes, you can be confident that you will gradually improve your skills or modify your behaviors.

3. Functional learning requires deep involvement.

A hallmark of Functional learning is its immersive, visceral nature. You are fully engaged; there's no desire to tune out, as when you are simply listening to a CD course or listening to a teacher speak. You are encouraged to develop and use your own critical thinking and problem-solving skills throughout the entire experience. This deep level of engagement, learning by doing, generates better retention of new concepts.

What's more, such visceral engagement helps drive you to succeed, both in the activity and in your professional and personal life. You engage in functional learning as yourself, so there's a level of personal investment present that doesn't exist when you are simply being asked to listen, for example. Because you are so personally invested, you're forced to take personal responsibility for the outcomes, as your practice shows the cause and effect of your behaviors. If you don't get the desired outcome in the functional learning exercise, you're probably seeing similar results in life, and then realize you will need to change your own behaviors to improve your results. Because functional learning mirrors reality, you now understand that if you aren't getting the results you want, you must change those behaviors, and take the next step of learning how to do so.

Functional learning temporarily takes you out of your real world, allows you to participate in a visceral experience, and results in learning that is memorable. This cycle has the potential to boost performance and significantly change behavior for improved results with a long-term impact.

Case Study: The Habit Loop: How Habits Work

In his excellent book *The Power of Habit: Why We Do What We Do in Life and Business*, Charles Duhigg explains how in the early 1990s, researchers from MIT started suspecting that a section of the brain called the basal ganglia might be key to habit formation. They realized that animals with injuries in the basal ganglia developed issues with routine tasks, such as learning how to run through a maze or remembering how to open a food container. The researchers decided to carry out an experiment that would allow them to examine, at minute scale, the changes and patterns occurring within the brains of rats while they performed dozens of pre-determined routines.

They put the rodents into a simple maze with a chocolate reward at the end. While each rat moved through the maze, the basal ganglia in its brain worked vigorously. When the rats sniffed the air or scratched the wall of the maze, their brain showed lots of activity, analyzing each new smell, texture, image and sound.

The scientists repeated this experiment hundreds of times, watching how each rat's brain reacted as it moved through the same maze repeatedly. A series of changes started to occur. After moving through the same routine hundreds of times, the rodents stopped smelling corners and walking the wrong way. They began to run through the maze faster and faster without stopping.

What was fascinating, however, was that as the rats learned how to move through the maze automatically, their brain activity decreased. As the routine became automatic, each rat went on autopilot and therefore started thinking less and less. The first few times the rats had to navigate the maze, they had to use their full effort to familiarize themselves with the challenge. They had to sniff, touch and scratch. They had to make decisions, make mistakes and then correct those mistakes to find the chocolate.

However, once they had repeated the same task enough, they did not need to scratch or sniff, or even make decisions about which way to go. Their brains had processed the maze so many times that the basal ganglia had mapped the whole process out for them. The parts of the brain associated with decision-making, smelling, and feeling had almost stopped, as they were no longer necessary. The rat's heart rates had also gone down, as they were no longer in an alien environment performing an alien (potentially dangerous) task. They no longer needed to think in order to navigate through the maze perfectly and get the reward at the end.

According to scientists, the results observed during this and many other similar studies, apply to other animals including humans. The brain automatically forms habits in order to save energy and become more efficient and successful at routine tasks needed for survival. Optimizing performance is in our DNA and our brains are constantly working towards this goal.

How to Form Positive Habits

The problem comes when we repeat negative or harmful behaviours or tasks, as the basal ganglia in our brain does not know the difference. The basal ganglia can and will automatically try to form habits if it sees an attractive reward at the end of the maze. For example, if you like the taste of donuts, any habit or process, which gets you donuts, will be an easy habit to form, as the basal ganglia will switch into habit formation mode, regardless of how bad donuts might be for your body. If you hate the taste of vegetables, the basal ganglia will not help you form a habit to get more vegetables into your body.

"This principle is why enjoyment in any form, is so important when it comes to increasing your emotional intelligence and business communication skills. Essentially, if you do not like something, you will not do it enough to form effective habits and your basal ganglia will not cooperate either. "

When you are trying to form new, positive habits like projecting your voice, improving your posture or exercising empathy, the trick is not to force yourself to do things you dislike, but to find things within your maze that you do like.

The Zone

"You can either love the process or love the goal."

If loving the goal that you want to achieve were enough, everybody would have six-pack abs and would be president of the world, with Ferraris and unicorns. Loving the goal is not enough, because your brain will not see a real reward at the end of the maze. It will see a long, unpleasant maze that it can easily get out of by just giving up.

"Most processes worth doing are very long, so you need to enjoy the journey"

The only way to achieve anything, from being healthier in the long-term, to getting fit, to achieving success in your career, is to actually enjoy the process of what you are doing more than the result or goal. When you live for the process and you cannot wait to get to work to practice your communication skills, then you will be "in the zone". Once you are in that zone, you will realize that your goals have changed and that your new goal is to be in the process and that the result is a nice side benefit to doing what you want. The world is there for you to take it, so start doing what you want today.

The Power of Dopamine Feedback Loops

Every process of your brain is heavily affected by your emotional state and the same is true for your audience. From what we know about the link between emotions and learning, we know that we learn best under specific conditions, particularly those that result in the release of dopamine. Dopamine is an incredible human motivator and is essentially the reason why gambling can be so addictive for some.

The neurotransmitter dopamine is responsible for delivering sensations of pleasure to the brain as a reward. The chemical is released naturally by the body when we experience success, and it plays a large role in why people become addicted to certain behaviors and substances. You can use dopamine to make your audience feel good and if you use it properly you can even influence them into developing positive habits.

Mark Lukens, Chairman for the Board for Behavioral Health Service North, a major behavioral health services provider in New York, explains that "dopamine is strongly connected to motivation, driving us to repeat the behaviors that create that rush, even when we aren't experiencing it." The actual dopamine rush may be short, but the brain remembers the feeling and how it got there.

The concept of the dopamine loop is what feeds addictions and progress alike. Repeating the same result over and over will still award dopamine, but in smaller quantities each time. In order to get the same rush, or an even larger one you need to up the stakes. For gamblers, this means increasing their wager, for addicts, it means increasing their dosage, and for others, it means seeking a greater challenge.

"Under the right circumstances, this can drive us to seek out ever-greater thrills," Lukens elaborates. This applies to everything from reaching the next level in a video game, to achieving more at work. Let's say it took you two weeks to gain 100 new followers for your business' social media account. You might aim to gain twice as many followers in half the time. Knowing what tasks will not only satisfy you, but your career as well will help you to focus on the important aspects at work.

If you're presenting information or training people, it's important to set up a series of small goals that all work together to create a greater success. Starting out with too large of a goal can actually hurt your ability to have an impact on your audience in the long-run, as failure won't create the dopamine rush which will motivate them to continue. Setting small benchmarks will not only help with focus, it'll keep you and your audience motivated with little hits of dopamine on the way to the big picture objective at the end. As with everything, it's important to balance long term objectives with short term goals.

"Your vision is your destination, and small, manageable goals are the motor that will get you there," explains Dr. Frank Murtha, New York-based counseling psychologist who focuses on investor psychology, behavioral finance and financial risk taking. "Without the vision you're on a road to nowhere. Without the goals, you have a destination but no motor. They work in tandem, and you need both."

We Learn More from Success than Failure

The age-old adage "learn from your mistakes" may need to be thrown away. Studies from The Picower Institute for Learning and Memory at MIT have shown that our learning brain cells are only active in situations where we succeed. Failure does not actually register on a physical level.

Continued success at an activity will help your brain to store the information that enabled that success for longer and thus allow you to learn and improve over time. Each success improves the connection between neurons and releases dopamine, which creates the dopamine loop to encourage your brain to repeat the successful behavior.

The effects of success and failure on the mind were confirmed in a study performed on monkeys where they were made to look at two images on a computer screen. When they looked at the correct image they were rewarded. Monkeys who received a reward for looking at the correct image in one trial were more likely to perform well on the following trial. There was little change in the monkey's who received no reward.

Similar observations have been made in humans, and though we can't make any assumptions, the study suggests that not only does our brain naturally change to adopt successful behaviors, but it barely changes at all when faced with failure.

How can you move faster towards your goals?

Michael Phelps was the most successful and most decorated Olympian of all time, with a total of 28 medals. Phelps also holds the all-time records for Olympic gold medals and Olympic gold medals in individual events among many other honors. He is a beast of success because he loved swimming and practiced it religiously to the detriment of all the other small stuff. He always put his "one big thing" first. We should all be more like Michael.

No more excuses, you must make doing the "one thing" a habit every day, and over the long-term, you will find that in 6 months you can achieve things that you thought were impossible.

Michael ate 12,000 calories a day. During intense training phases, Michael swam a minimum of 80,000 meters a week, which is nearly 50 miles. Michael is now retired, but as a professional swimmer, he lived his life by one rule and one rule only. "Will it make me swim faster?" "I fancy a pizza and an evening on the sofa so should I skip training?" "Will doing that make me swim faster?. "No." "Will training make me swim faster?"- "YES, I´m going out to train".

Quick-Notes: EQ & Leadership at Work

The importance of understanding your own emotions and being sure about your purpose is self-awareness. Self-management flows from this principle. It's an unhindered drive to be on track. You can't control your emotions if you don't understand what you're feeling. Otherwise, your emotions end up controlling you.

Fear is your ally, you'd be dead without it

Negative emotions can feel overwhelming. This is how the brain alerts us of a potential threat, but your mind often misinterprets the message. If your brain warns you of a potential threat, it's paving the way towards fight or flight, but it doesn't mean that fight or flight is needed, it's just warning you of the possibility of danger.

If fear or negative emotions make you lose focus of the duty at hand by hijacking your mental state you increase the chances of that danger becoming a reality. It could be news of a drop in market shares, news of layoffs or any other upsetting or potentially dangerous information.

Self-management is like an ongoing inner dialog. It's a part of emotional intelligence, which liberates you from internalizing your feelings. It clears a path towards clarity and focused energy. It prevents distressing emotions from pushing you off track and increasing the likelihood of disaster.

Your emotional leakage has public consequences.

Remember that emotions are contagious and are communicated through our body language and our voice more than our words. To help others manage their emotion, you must first learn to deal with your own. This doesn't mean that you get to escape the stresses of life. A death, divorce, illness of a loved one or a detached child can influence anyone massively, but you need to manage the fallout.

If you express your anger freely or let your negative emotions run wild, you can't lead communicate effectively because you're no longer in control of yourself. The brain performs a pivotal role; basically, a person with stronger self-management

Self-Awareness

In simple terms, self-awareness is the ability to understand your own emotions in practice, be it strength or weakness and values or motives. People with strong self-awareness are realistic to the point where they are truthful to themselves and others about their own strengths and weaknesses. Their impartial honesty about themselves and the world gives them power and confidence, which lets them learn from their own mistakes and see them within 'the bigger picture'. They see their professional life as a journey without a final destination.

Perhaps the most obvious indication of a self-aware person is the tendency to find time to introspect by themselves, which allows them to reorganize their thoughts.

Self-aware people in business use planning and goalsetting as a habit to give them a clear-cut understanding of their visions, principles, and aims. They know how to stay on track by being attuned to the right feelings. They plan and strategize their goals before taking massive decisive action towards them. They are realistic and know that they need to work hard in order to be successful at anything.

For example, despite the financial issues, they are willing to reject a job that doesn't conform to their ideals. On the other hand, a person who lacks self-awareness is likely to be in a situation where they sign up for the job for the money and lose interest in two years.

How does this affect a business or a leader of an organization?

We often make a common mistake of perceiving motivation as black and white and is taken for granted, but there is a lot of grey in between. The usual assumption is that people care about the work they do. Wherever the work role gravitates us, is where the point of interest lies - and that in itself is motivating. Traditional inducements include appreciation or bonuses that make one perform better, but no number of external motivators can make anyone be at their absolute best in terms of performance.

The Open Loop System

E. I competencies are not talents but acquired abilities, each with a connection to the behavior of the more efficient resonant leader.

Scientists have described the emotional intelligence centers in the brain as 'the open loop system' or 'emotional centers'. A 'closed-loop system', like the circulatory system, is self-regulating. It does not impact other people's circulatory system. The open loop system is dependent on external triggers. We depend on external stimuli to maintain our emotional strength. From an evolutionary perspective, it has kept humans together and allowed us to form societies, which require participation and teamwork. The open loop system has kept people together for emotional relief and strength for thousands of years.

Research suggests that emotional intelligence caters to committing to a basic strategy, building relationships that offer competitive advantage, encouraging innovation, providing a platform for shared learning, maintaining balance between the human side and financial side of the company's agenda, and developing open communication and trust.

It's Just a Set of Skills

Emotional intelligence is not a single character or ability but an array of distinct mental reasoning abilities: Perceiving, Regulating and Understanding emotions.

- Perceiving emotions include the distinguishing and processing of the meaning of certain mental states and linking it to other sensory experiences.

- Understanding emotion is about the detection of how basic emotions merge to form complex emotions, how surrounding incidents affect emotions and if certain reactions are in the considered social setting.

- Regulating emotions consists of controlling emotions of oneself and others.

Emotional intelligence is a set of skills that result in the ability to understand and regulate your own and others people's emotions and to use this information to guide your thought patterns and behavior. In other words, anyone with emotional intelligence is aware of their own emotions and those of others and can express both positive and negative emotions and internal feelings when appropriate and have an impact on other people's moods.

The Mixed Model

The four dimensions of emotional intelligence was a model created by Daniel Goleman in 1988. It is known as the mixed model. It has four divisions and eighteen competencies.

Self-Awareness

- Emotional self-awareness - reading one's thoughts and finding their impact.

- Accurate self-assessment - identifying one's boundaries and strengths.

- Self-confidence- knowing self-worth and abilities.

Self-Management

- Emotional self-control -control of impulses and emotions.

- Transparency -practicing dignity and truthfulness.

- Adaptability - flexibility to adapt to situations depending on obstacles.

- Achievement -the willpower to improve abilities to reach one's standard of excellence.

- Initiative - eagerness to capture opportunities.

- Optimism - ability to see past the downside of events.

Social –Awareness

- Empathy-comprehending others' perspective and emotions to act on their concerns.

- Organizational awareness - interest in understanding politics and networks at the organizational level.

- Service -meeting the needs of fellow employees and clients.

Relationship Management

- Inspirational leadership - directing and encouraging with a solid vision

- Influence - using various techniques of persuasion.

- Developing others -improving the confidence of others by commenting and directing

- Change catalyst - triggering to move in a new direction

- Conflict management - resolution of conflicts

- Teamwork and collaboration

The Five Discoveries:

Five essential questions you need to answer before you can embark on your mission to improve your communication skills and use your personality to your advantage.

Exercise

Take a clean notebook or a sheet of paper and write down your answers to the following questions:

Discovery one: my ideal self, who do I aspire to be?

Discovery two: my real self, who am I? What strengths and limits do I possess?

Discovery three: my learning scheme - how can I develop my strengths while overcoming my limitations

Discovery four: trying out and practicing new behaviors to the point of mastery. What should I practice and where or how should I practice it?

Discovery five: building nurturing and responsible relationships that make lasting changes possible. Who are my closest relationships? Are they nurturing and positive? If not, how can I change this? What type of relationships do I want, and how can I create them?

Bibliography:

AAP (1998) Learning disabilities, dyslexia, and vision: A subject review (electronic version), Pediatrics. American Academy of Pediatrics.

AACAP (1997) Practice parameters for the assessment and treatment of children, adolescents, and adults with attention-deficit hyperactivity disorder. Journal of the American Academy of Child and Adolescent Psychiatry, 36, 85S–121S.

Abdullaev, Y. G. and Posner, M. I. (1997) Time course of activating brain areas in generating verbal associations. Psychological Science, 8, 56–59.

Abrahams, E., Ginsburg, G. S. and Silver, M. (2005) The personalized medicine coalition: Goals and strategies. American Journal of Pharmacogenomics, 5, 345–355.

Acevedo, A. and Loewenstein, D. A. (2007) Nonpharmacological cognitive interventions in aging and dementia. Journal of Geriatric Psychiatry and Neurology, 20, 239–249.

Adcock, R. A. (2006) Reward-motivated learning: mesolimbic activation precedes memory formation. Neuron, 50, 507–517.

Adolphs, R., Tranel, D. and Damasio, A. R. (2003) Dissociable neural systems for recognizing emotions. Brain and Cognition, 52, 61–69.

AERA (2000) Ethical Standards of the American Educational Research Association. Ahamed, Y., MacDonald, H., Reed, K.,

Beauchamp, M. S., Lee, K. E., Argall, B. D. and Martin, A. (2004) Integration of auditory and visual information about objects in superior temporal sulcus. Neuron, 41, 809–823.

Blackwell, Lisa S., Kali H. Trzesniewski, and Carol Sorich Dweck. "Implicit Theories of Intelligence Predict Achievement Across an Adolescent Transition: A Longitudinal Study and an Intervention." Child Development 78, no. 1 (2007): 246-63. doi:10.1111/j.1467-8624.2007.00995.x.

Blakemore, S. J., Samuel, E., Summers, I. R. and Claxton, G. (2005) Semantic divergence and creative story generation: An fMRI investigation. Cognitive Brain Research, 25, 240–250.

Bradberry T. & Greaves J. (2009) Emotional intelligence 2.0, Har/Dol En edition edn., TalentSmart.

Covey Stephen R, (2013), The 7 Habits of Highly Effective People: Powerful Lessons in Personal Change, Simon & Schuster

Duhigg, Charles. The Power of Habit: Why We Do What We Do in Life and Business. Toronto: Anchor Canada, 2014.

Draganski, B., Gaser, C., Busch, V., Schuierer, G., Bogdahn, U. and May, A. (2004) Changes in grey matter induced by training. Nature, 427, 311–312.

Elkins, J. S., Longstreth, W. T., Manolio, T. A., Newman, A. B., Bhadelia, R. A. and Johnston, S. C. (2006) Education and the cognitive decline associated with MRI-defined brain infarct. Neurology, 67, 435–440.

Gardner, H. (1983) Frames of the Mind: The Theory of Multiple Intelligences. New York: Basic Books.

Good, C. D., Ashburner, J., Frackowiak, R. S. and Frith, C. D. (2000) Navigation related structural change in the hippocampi of taxi drivers. Proceedings of the National Academy of Sciences (USA), 97, 4398–4403.

Hillis, & E., A. (2013, November 30). Inability to empathize: Brain lesions that disrupt sharing and understanding another's emotions. Retrieved from https://academic.oup.com/brain/article/137/4/981/365719

Huttenlocher, P. R. and Dabholkar, A. S. (1997) Regional differences in synaptogenesis in human cerebral cortex. Journal of Comparative Neurology, 387, 167–178.

Joels, M., Pu, Z. W., Wiegert, O., Oitzl, M. S. and Krugers, H. J. (2006) Learning under stress: How does it work? Trends in Cognitive Sciences, 10, 152–158.

Kuhl, P. K., Williams, K. A., Lacerda, F., Stevens, K. N. and Lindblom, B. (1992) Linguistic experience alters phonetic perception in infants by 6 months of age. Science, 255, 606–608.

Leclerc, C. M. and Hess, T. M. (2007) Age differences in the bases for social judgments: Tests of a social expertise perspective. Experimental Aging Research, 33, 95–120.

Lopes, P. N., Salovey, P., & Straus, R. (2003). Emotional Intelligence, Personality and the Perceived Quality of Social Relationships. The Journal of Personality and Individual Differences, 35(3), 641–658.

Morrison, J. H. and Hof, P. R. (1997) Life and death of neurons in the aging brain. Science, 278, 412–419.

Olff, M., Langeland, W. and Gersons, B. P. R. (2005) The psychobiology of PTSD: coping with trauma. Psychoneuroendocrinology, 30, 974–982.

Ong, Vanessa. "15 Bad Speeches We Can Learn From." HighSpark. Last modified December 11, 2017. https://highspark.co/15-bad-speeches-avoid-in-presentations/

Paivio, A. and Csapo, K. (1973) Picture superiority in free recall: imagery or dual coding? Cognitive Psychology, 5, 176–206.

Quervain, D. J. F., Roozendaal, B., Nitsch, R. M., McGaugh, J. L. and Hock, C. (2000) Acute cortisone administration impairs retrieval of long-term declarative memory in humans. Nature Neuroscience, 3, 313–314.

Shane L. Rogers, Oliver Guidetti, Craig P. Speelman, Melissa Longmuir, Ruben Phillips. Contact Is in the Eye of the Beholder: The Eye Contact Illusion. Perception, 2019; 030100661982748 DOI: 10.1177/0301006619827486

Scheff, S. W., Price, D. A. and Sparks, D. L. (2001) Quantitative assessment of possible age-related change in synaptic numbers in the human frontal cortex. Neurobiology of Aging, 22, 355–365.

Shors, T. J., Miesegaes, G., Beylin, A., Zhao, M. R., Rydel, T. and Gould, E. (2001) Neurogenesis in the adult is involved in the formation of trace memories Nature, 414, 938–938.

Sowell, E. R., Peterson, B. S., Thompson, P. M., Welcome, S. E., Henkenius, A. L. and Toga, A. W. (2003) Mapping cortical change across the human life span. Nature Neuroscience, 6(3), 309–315.

Strickland, D.S. (2000). Emotional intelligence: the most potent factor in the success equation. The Journal of nursing administration, 30 3, 112-7.

The Economist (2010). The Economist Style Guide. PUBLICAFFAIRS; 12th Edition

Wilson, R. S. (2005) Mental challenge in the workplace and risk of dementia in old age: is there a connection? Occupational and Environmental Medicine, 62, 72–73.

Resources: 6 Videos on Emotional Intelligence

The Power of Emotional Intelligence – Travis Bradberry

https://www.youtube.com/watch?v=auXNnTmhHsk

You aren't at the mercy of your emotions – your brain creates them – Lisa Feldman Barrett

https://www.youtube.com/watch?v=0gks6ceq4eQ

6 Steps to Improve Your Emotional Intelligence – Ramona Hacker

https://www.youtube.com/watch?v=D6_J7FfgWVc

Learning Human Values Via Emotional Intelligence – Ruby Bakshi Khurdi

https://www.youtube.com/watch?v=4YCAo8kxOHs

Your Forensic Mirror: Applying Emotional Intelligence To Achieve Success – Paula Clarke

https://www.youtube.com/watch?v=McG6tETL93s

The People Currency: Practicing Emotional Intelligence – Jason Bridges

https://www.youtube.com/watch?v=7z0asInbu24

Free Bonus: 300+ Presentation Templates for PowerPoint

Here, you will find a downloadable database of 300+ Premium PowerPoint presentation templates, which you can use or edit as you please.

https://drive.google.com/open?id=1oArc1iu3xJSgspmOK6PYRpVuk3F_Wqsh

Sign up for our free resource newsletter, to receive more free resources! ☺

I hope you have found this book useful. Thank you for reading.

https://www.idmadrid.es/vip-resources

Bonus Chapter: The Productivity Cheat Sheet

Download your free copy of The Productivity Cheat Sheet: 15 Secrets of Productivity here!

https://www.idmadrid.es/vip-resources

Thank you

If you enjoyed this emotional intelligence and business communication or found it useful, I'd be very grateful if you'd post a short review on Amazon.

Your support really does make a difference and means a lot to me. I read all the reviews personally so I can get your feedback and make this book even better in the future.

Thanks again for your support!

www.ingramcontent.com/pod-product-compliance
Lightning Source LLC
Chambersburg PA
CBHW031140250726

48655CB00002B/770